Hacking

————— ❧❧❧❧❧ —————

What EVERY Beginner Needs to Know

Table of Contents

Introduction

Hacking is an interesting art form that requires a user to possess a solid understanding of how computers work. Many of us may be conditioned to regard a hacker as a criminal, someone who has obtained unauthorized information and is using it in unethical ways to their own advantage. However, you may be surprised to discover that there is so much more to it than that. Sure, there are some unethical hackers that will engage in the behaviors described above, but there are many who will learn how to hack solely for the benign purpose of protecting themselves, their family members, or a business that they are associated with. There are also users who are attempting to gain access into an unauthorized system simply because they are curious and not because they desire to engage in malicious activities or some type of sabotage.

BONUS:

Revolutionary Credit Repair Secrets

And as a special thank you to my readers, my co-author Michael McCord- has graciously agreed to give away copies of his book- **Revolutionary Credit Repair Secrets- Cardinal Rules to Get You a Perfect Credit Score.** You will receive outstanding tips to improve your credit score and your financial health.

To get instant access to this book and more awesome resources, check out the link below:

CLICK HERE

https://mccordpublishing.leadpages.co/computers-and-technology/

As an added bonus, subscribers will be given a chance to get exclusive sneak peeks of upcoming books on Computers and Technology and discounts that will not be available to the general public. You will also have the opportunity to obtain free copies of my subsequent books with no strings attached. Don't worry, we treat your e-mail with the respect it deserves. We will not spam you and that's a promise!

What You Will Find In this Hacking Book

The world of hacking is interesting and also exceedingly complex. This guidebook will take a look at hacking and all the various components that it entails. We will look at what hacking is, how it has evolved since the 1960s and the different manners in which hacking has been utilized over time.

After gaining a good understanding of hacking and an awareness of how it works, you will be prepared to learn some of the basics of hacking. Afterwards, you will be geared up to engage in some fairly basic hacking activities yourself. There are many reasons that you may want to hack, many of which don't require any mischief on your part. One such reason may be your understandable desire to secure and protect your personal information. Having the correct plan and the right strategies to do so will make this task much easier and much safer to accomplish.

Even as a beginner, you can easily learn how to hack. It's not rocket science and it's a Hollywood myth that you need to be a brilliant techno-genius to be able to hack effectively. This guidebook will provide the road map and the strategies that you need to get started with this worthwhile endeavor.

Since this is a beginner's book, the strategies we will show you may not be the most sophisticated options out there, but conversely they will also be less risky than some of the techniques more advanced hackers implement. In time though you can easily reach a more advanced level based on your personal goals, desires, and work ethic. Overall, we will show you how to get started with hacking and we will help you get the information that you want to start learning like a professional.

Additionally, if you are interested in going beyond the world of Hacking and diving into Computer Programming, we have numerous books that cover this topic. We have guides on **Python, JavaScript and SQL.** Additionally, for anyone interested in surfing the Internet anonymously, we still soon have a great book on **TOR and Anonymous Internet Surfing.**

Please visit our Amazon Author Page to check out guides like these:

<u>CLICK HERE</u>

https://www.amazon.com/Mark-Anderson/e/B01N51MTHL/ref=dp_byline _cont_ebooks_1

CLICK HERE

https://www.amazon.com/JavaScript-EVERY-Beginner-Programming-Activate-ebook/dp/B01MSM5NZK

CLICK HERE

https://www.amazon.com/SQL-EVERY-Beginner-Development-Programming-ebook/dp/B01MSLLTYR/

If you check out our Programming Library, you WILL increase your earning capacity and marketability at any company dramatically. You will confidently walk into any interview knowing that your skill sets **will be valued** and you have something unique to bring to the table. So don't miss out!!

You don't need to have a degree in computer sciences or have worked with computers all your life in order to get started on hacking. Some people do have those things under their belt and while it is certainly an advantage, it is not a prerequisite. You simply need to have an interest in computers and the ability to learn. So let's get started with learning about hacking and how to put it to good use for yourself to successfully achieve your desired outcomes.

Chapter 1:

Introduction to Hacking

We have all heard about hackers thanks to our media and the way that Hollywood likes to portray them in movies. We think of someone who is smart and sits in their basement while getting onto any network that they choose. It is exciting when we watch movies and the media portray hacking in their own ways, but neither Hollywood nor the mainstream press really shows the true story of hacking.

The term hacker came up during the 1960s and was originally used to describe a programmer or someone who was able to hack out a computer code. These people were able to see future ways to use a computer and would create new programs that no one else could. They were basically innovators in their fields at the time and they would ultimately end up being the ones who led the computer industry to where it is today.

These early hackers were interested in their work. They were excited to create a new program, but they wanted to learn how other systems worked as well. If there happened to be a bug in another system, these hackers would be the ones who would create patches that could help fix the problem.

While at first these people were visionaries that helped to create programs and even fix what wasn't working for others, things started to change once the computer system started going over into networks. Then the term hacker would expand to be seen as someone who was able to get onto a network where their access was restricted. Sometimes this hacker may have been on a particular network because they were curious to find out how it worked and other times it was for more malicious intents and purposes.

As you can see, there is a big difference between what was seen as a hacker a few decades ago and what is seen as a hacker today. Some of this confusion exists because there are two sides to hacking- which we will analyze in more detail later- and each one will work slightly differently to either expose or protect the network in question.

The process of hacking is something that is often in the news, but most people don't understand what it is all about. Basically, hacking is the process of modifying the software and hardware of a computer to accomplish a goal that was outside its original purpose. It can also include any time that someone enters into a network that they are not allowed. Those who engage in this process are known as hackers and they are often able to get onto computers, systems, and find access to information they may not be authorized to.

While the media may lead us to believe that all hackers are up to no good, for the majority of them, this is just not the case. Some just see it as a challenge and an adrenaline rush to get onto a system, even if they shouldn't. Others enjoy learning about computers and figuring out what they are able to do. Most of the hacking that goes on today is not meant to be destructive or criminal at all, although the law may look at these things differently.

Since many hackers are considered computer prodigies, there are actually quite a few corporations in America who employ them on their technical staff. These hackers are able to work with the company to figure out any flaws present in the security system, making it easier to fix these problems before a criminal hacker gets in. These individuals can help stop identity theft, protect the organization, and so much more.

In addition, computer hacking has led to other developments in technology. One such example is Dennis Ritchie, a former hacker, who created the UNIX operating system, which had a big impact on how Linux was later developed. Shawn Fanning, who is the creator of Napster, is also known as a computer hacker as well as a leader in technology.

Of course, it is those with less noble motives for hacking that are the ones that get the most intention. Some are out to steal your personal information, break into a company's information, and get onto a network without the proper authorization. This is a criminal offence and can land you in jail for 20 years as well as have you paying many hefty fines. These are the types of people that have brought about heavier laws against hacking, more stringent anti-virus and malware, and more.

As you can see, there are many sides to the hacking world. Most hackers are just really interested in computers and have the ability to put this knowledge to work in the technology field while others are less noble and will work to get onto networks and steal information that is not theirs.

Common Terms to Know

Now that you have an idea of what hacking is about, it is important to know some of the common terms that come about in the hacking word. Make sure to look over some of these terms and understand them because that will make it much easier to absorb the information in the following chapters.

- Adware—adware is a type of software that is designed to make pre-selected adds come on your software. Some of it will be malicious and will take over your computer and slow down your system, tying up resources and making it impossible to use the computer how you want.

- Back door—this is a point of entry into a computer or system that will circumvent normal security and is often used to access a computer system or network. The system developer may have created this as a shortcut during the developmental stage, but if they forget to remove it, hackers can get it. Sometimes, the hacker is able to create their own back door into the system.

- Black hat—this is the bad guy, the hacker that wants to use the information in a bad way. They may also share this information with other black hats to exploit the system.

- Cookies—this is a bit of information that a website will store in your computer browser about your search history. It can save time when filling out forms on a site and so on. A hacker could get this information and use it if you don't delete on occasion.

- Cracker—these are the hackers that use their skills to get onto sites and networks illegally, usually to cause harm.

- Firewall—this is a barrier on the system that helps keep unwanted intruders away from the network. These can be either a software or a physical device and if it is designed well, it can keep hackers out.

- Gray hat—this is a hybrid between white hat and black hat. They usually work to expose flaws that are in the security of the system. They may use some illegal means to do so, but can help to protect an individual or company in the process, sometimes even working for that company.

- Key logger—this program won't destroy your computer, but it will log every stroke that you make on the computer. The information can be sent back to a black hat who will use it to determine your username and password to use later. This can put your banking information, private information, and even social media at risk. Often this is combined with a screenshot hack so that the hacker has better access to what sites you are visiting when you type in your information.

- Malware—this is a malicious program that will cause damage and can include things like logic bombs, time bombs, worms, viruses, and Trojans.

- Phishing—this is when you receive a message, usually in email, that looks legitimate, but is from a black hat who is trying to get personal information. You may receive something that looks like it comes from your bank, for example, asking for your name, address, PIN, and social security number. Remember that banks and other institutions will never ask for this online. A good way to stay safe with these emails is to never click on the link directly in the email. Go to your search browser and type in the website and visit from there.

- Virus—this is a malicious code or program that will attach to another program file and even replicate itself to infect other systems. It is kind of like the flu in that it will spread around and infect many systems at once. It can be spread using a networked system, a memory stick, CD, or through email.

- White hat—these are hackers that use their skills for ethical purposes. They may use them to thwart off a black hat and keep the computer system working properly. Many companies will hire white hats to keep their system running properly.

- Man in the middle attack—this is when the hacker will insert themselves into the network in order to watch traffic and change the messages that are being sent. The system will see them as legitimate and the targets often don't realize that their messages and traffic are being manipulated. When the first computer sends information, it will go to the hacker computer, who can then make changes to the information, or just read it through to learn about the network, before sending it on to the intended receiver. Both the receiver and the sender will assume that the hacker should be there if the man in the middle attack works successfully.

- Brute force attack—this is a tactic that can take a bit of time since it will use all combinations of letter, numbers, and characters to get onto a system. It is inefficient, but it does work and is often saved for when all other alternatives are not working.

- Denial of service attack—this is an attack that is used to make a network or website unresponsive. It is often achieved when the hacker sends a huge amount of content requests so that there is an overload to the server. While the server is unresponsive, the hacker is able to get in and get the information that they want.

- IP—this is the internet protocol address. It is the fingerprint that every device will carry to help it to connect. If the hacker has the IP address of a device, they are able to find out where it is located, track any activity on it, and even find out who is using the computer.

These are just a few of the terms that you may come across when dealing with the hacking world. There are many other terms of attacks that black hats can perform on computer systems in order to receive information they want, take over the computer and more. Understanding the various methods of attack and learning how hacking works can help you to understand the many different aspects of the hacking world.

Common Misconceptions About Hacking

Hacking has been around for some time and because of the media and what you have heard about the process, you may have some misconceptions about what this process is about. Here we will explore some of the common misconceptions with hacking to develop a better understanding.

Hacking is always illegal

When you read an article online or in a newspaper about hacking, it is usually in regards to the illegal hacking where someone got onto a network they weren't supposed to and caused mayhem or hackers that spread malware and viruses. These types of hacking are illegal, but that doesn't mean that all hacking is illegal.

There is a type of hacking called ethical hacking. These are people who work for companies to help them expose flaws in the system, those who work to keep others out, and so on. These people will help to protect networks and systems for companies and individuals, rather than using them for evil purposes.

All hackers are young

Another misconception that you may come across is that all hackers are young, either they are teenagers or in their early 20s. While there are some hackers who fit into this age range, hackers are anyone who knows a lot about computers and how to get into places they may not be allowed in. Often younger hackers are the ones who are caught doing illegal hacking because they are younger with less experience, but anyone of any age can be a hacker.

Security software will stop hacking

Having a security system in place may help to keep your computer safe from some threats, but it is not always a safe way to protect from all hackers. Hackers are often able to get through this software in order to get your sensitive information. Plus, often the issue isn't because of the software, but because the user does something wrong. Hackers are going to use tricks and other ways to convince you to let them in to your system, regardless of the software you have on your computer.

For example, you may have the best security system on your computer, but if you click on a link and hand over the information, the hackers still won. Many times hackers will send emails or information looking like someone else, like your bank, and request this personal information. Those who aren't paying attention will send out the information and expose themselves to the hacker, regardless of their security software.

Hacking Needs, a lot of software

Thanks to Hollywood, there are many rumors and misconceptions that come with hacking and one of these is that you need special software, sometimes obtained illegally, in order to hack onto other systems. But in reality, you only need some simple tools to get it done. For example, you can use a Web application for hacking that will take a look at different websites and find the vulnerabilities that are on them. White hat hackers will use these to help find the mistakes and make the website safer, but the black hat hackers will go through this to exploit the website.

For the most part, hacking is about trying lots of different things, just a bit differently, until you find a way that breaks the system. You won't need the most exotic software to do this, but you will need some horsepower on the computer and a lot of patience to get it done.

You need an advanced degree to be a hacker

Some hackers do have an advanced degree for their jobs. These are the ones who maybe have a love for computers and work for a big company to find flaws in the system. They went to school to help get their foot in the door and to ensure that they knew the latest technology in hacking to help out others.

Becoming a hacker does not require years of education. In fact, many of the best hackers have never gone to college at all, or at least not for a computer related study. You just need to have a love for computers and the ability to learn how they work. You can easily learn how to do a lot of the work with hacking from your own home and many of those who get into the hacking field go this way rather than through college.

Chapter 2:

Ethical Hacking vs. Criminal Hacking

There are two worlds when it comes to hacking. There are those who will use their hacking skills to help out others. They may do it in their free time and find loopholes or back doors in a corporate website and alert that company in order to help them. Some of these individuals even work for hospitals, corporations, and other companies with the sole purpose of finding and fixing any low points in security to keep personal information safe. They may hack through the system, but they do it in an ethical way to help out.

The other world is a bit darker and is full of hackers that use their skills for their own personal advantages. They may hack through a system to get personal information. They can send emails and links requesting personal information for identity theft and other mischief. They are not helping out anyone but themselves in this process.

Each of these worlds will work the same when it comes to hacking and using the same tools, but they will do so for different reasons. While the media will spend most of their time looking at the black hat hacking- those who get in trouble for their endeavors- there is a whole world of ethical hacking that is doing a lot of good in the world and saving people a lot of money, time, and headaches in the long run.

Ethical Hacking

Ethical hackers are going to use a lot of the same techniques and methods as criminal hackers to get past the defenses in place for a network, but they are going to do so for different reasons. Ethical hackers go past the security systems in order to document these loopholes and provide some advice on how to fix these issues. Many of them will work for the corporation that has the website so they can make the documentation and help to put a plan in place to fix the issue. Others may just find out about the loophole and will notify the company, without having any affiliation with them.

The idea behind ethical hacking is to check out the security of a network. The company understands that there are hackers out there who may want to get on the network and steal personal information. When it comes to online stores, hospitals, and other companies, there can be a lot of personal information for a wide range of clients. If a black hat gets in, this information is freely available and thousands of people could be affected.

Knowing this information, companies will hire white hats to help locate any vulnerabilities that will be in their system. They will also spend time trying to figure out whether any malicious activities could happen within the software in the future. These vulnerabilities are often going to be found in improper system configurations, such as a software flaw, and the white hat will work to get them fixed up to protect that valuable information.

Pretty much any company that has their connection over the internet and holds personal information of their clients on the database should consider having a white hat help them out, or at least someone who has knowledge of basic hacking. This will help them take care of the vulnerabilities a bit better and will make it easier to protect their customers.

Chapter 2: Ethical Hacking vs. Criminal Hacking

While hacking has been around for a bit, it wasn't until the 1970s when the first ethical hacking process began. The United States realized that they were in possession of a lot of personal information and that black hats would love to get this information. The government decided to call in experts, who were known as red teams, to hack into the computer systems and find where any vulnerabilities were. This soon became a big industry within the information security market and many big corporations now include this kind of work in their infrastructure to keep safe.

Now that so much personal information is being shared over the internet, there are various standards in place that require all organizations that connect to the internet to have a penetration test. This is basically a test that the organization has to go through to ensure that their information is safe and that the loopholes are all taken care of. Smaller organizations may hire an ethical hacker to help out with this on occasion to keep up to date and bigger companies will have whole teams that work for them full time to keep intruders out.

There are many ways that an ethical hacker can help out their clients and it is becoming a growing field. While many people still feel that a hacker is someone who is only up to mischief or interested in stealing information, there are many more hackers who work in an ethical way to help keep computer networks safe. They may use some of the same techniques as their black hat counterparts, but they use them for good rather than evil.

Ethical hacking has grown in popularity and has been a great way for organizations to take their security into their own hands. A white hat hacker will work for the company to go through the hacking process to help keep clients' information safe from unscrupulous people. Some security professionals go by different names because they don't like the correlation with "hacker" but they work in a similar manner- for the purpose of helping out.

Criminal Hacking

The other side of hacking is a bit darker. Rather than trying to protect the personal information of others and to help a company stay safe, a criminal hacker steals the information for their own personal use. They may get into a company's network in order to steal emails and credit card numbers to use as their own. They may send a virus around or ask for information, pretending to be someone else, to harm the other person and help themselves.

Basically, criminal hacking is any act that is committed by someone who has a lot of knowledge of computers who will then use their information to accomplish various acts of intellectual property theft, identity theft, credit card fraud, vandalism, terrorism, and other crimes on the computer. It will often infringe on the privacy of the other person or groups of people and can even cause some damage to a computer based property. There are a lot of reasons that criminal hacking will happen, but often it is to see a financial gain for the hacker.

There are several ways a criminal hacker can get onto the network and find personal information they can use maliciously. Viruses are a popular option that can get on your computer and will send the information back to the original sender. Trojan horses will get to your computer because they look like a legitimate program but are often providing an easy backdoor for the hacker to get into your system. Other programs can quietly add on to your computer and will document your keystrokes in order to figure out your username and passwords to emails, banking sites, and more.

Another method that many black hat hackers will use is to send emails. These emails will look like they come from legitimate sites, such as your bank, and will have links inside. If you click the link, you may end up with a virus or another issue on the computer. Some will even go so far as to send you a form asking for personal information. If you provide the information, you will find that it goes straight to the hacker and the request was never from your bank or the source it claimed.

There is a lot of damage that can be caused by black hat hackers, especially if an individual or company is not taking the right steps to ensure there is computer safety around them. People could lose a lot of money, have to deal with identity theft, and so much more. It is a good idea to always keep a vigilant eye out to find when these breaches could be happening.

There are some cases of famous hackers over the last few decades. For example, David Smith is one of the most notable of these cases when he launched the Melissa Virus in 1999. This virus was able to get to 1.2 million computers and businesses in Europe and the United States lost $80 million. Once he was caught, Smith was convicted of criminal hacking and had a sentence of forty years. He was released after just shy of two years in prison after agreeing to work for the FBI.

This is just one of the cases of criminal hacking and most of them will not happen so widespread as the one above. Still, they cost millions of dollars in financial losses each year to many businesses when a "black hat" hacker is able to get onto a computer and take this personal information.

There is basically a race between the black hat and white hat hackers. The white hats are working to close up all the loopholes and back doors that they can find on networks and other computers and the black hats are trying to get in before things are closed or find a new way to cause a mess. Sometimes the white hats win and can keep people out, but there are many times when a black hat will be able to beat them to it and will do their damage.

White hat and black hat hackers will use a lot of the same techniques in order to take over a computer system. They will be able to get onto the systems in the same way, look at the information, and complete the same tasks. The difference in that an ethical hacker is going to do this in order to find vulnerabilities in a network in order to fix them while a criminal hacker is more interested in finding out personal information, causing loss for a company, and causing other mischief with their work.

Chapter 3:

Passive and Active Attacks

There are many different attacks that a hacker can perform on your computer. It is often going to depend on the kind of information they would like to get from the network and how active they are planning on being in all the work. Here are some of the ways that a hacker can attempt to get onto the system.

All types of attacks that a hacker can perform will fit into two categories; passive attacks and active attacks. Passive attacks are often seen as research since the hacker will get onto the system but won't cause any damage until later after they have time to look around. Active attacks are the ones where the hacker has learned about the system and is ready to do their damage. Let's look at the differences between these two attacks and how the hacker will work with each one.

Passive Attacks

A passive attack is when where the hacker is going to wait for the right opportunity to get onto your system and cause havoc. The hacker may get onto your system, and then waits a bit before performing their attack. This is usually a good way for the hacker to get onto and then observe your network, the software that is used, and what security measures you have in place before starting their attack.

The passive attacks are the ones that will happen when a hacker will monitor to find the vulnerabilities in a system without making any changes in your system. It is basically a way for the hacker to research your system, without you knowing, so their attacks are more effective. There are several different types ways that you can classify these types of attacks.

1. Active reconnaissance—by using port scanning, the intruder is able to listen to the targeted system and then engage it to find where any weak points are. It is effective for finding the vulnerable spots and then the hacker will be able to engage these weak points and exploit them.

2. Passive reconnaissance—this is when the hacker is going to sit back and just study the system without actively engaging the system. It can include masquerading, dumpster diving, and war driving.

These are two tactics that are great tools when the hacker wants to find the vulnerabilities in a computer system so that you can prevent the attacks later on. Once you use the reconnaissance tactics, you will be able to see where any weak points are located. You may also find that installing an intrusion prevention system, or IPS, will help to protect your automated methods, port scans, and more on the system.

Active Attacks

Active attacks are meant to get onto a system and take over the information. They can cause more immediate harm to the system because the hacker is actively trying to get information and take things that don't belong to them. The network often won't know that the hacker is there, but the hacker will be able to get in and cause whatever issues they would like. Some examples of active attacks that are common include:

Masquerade attack

With this attack, the hacker is going to pretend to be a user of the network. They will be able to trick the system into thinking they have authorization to gain access to private files and information. Sometimes the hacker will be able to do this through back door methods but often it is from gaining passwords and user IDs or exploiting a security flaw.

Once the hacker is able to get onto the system, they will be able to do everything that a regular user can on the system. They can make changes to the software, delete files, kick out other users on the network, and more.

Session replay

With this attack, the hacker is going to get onto the system to create automatic authentication each time the target goes onto a particular website. This attack will be able to exploit the nature of the web for storing URLs, cookies, and forms in a browser. When the hacker gets this data, the hacker can then do a session replay attack the hacker can effectively work of the system like everyone else.

The session replay attack is not going to happen on real time so this can make it hard for the legitimate user to catch. Often, it is only found when the user fins there are discrepancies on their account of some kind. Often, it is only found once identity theft has occurred and the user will have to go through and try to get it all fixed.

Denial of Service and Distributed Denial of Service

When talking about a DoS attack is when the hacker will deny service or access to someone who is an actual legitimate user of the system. You will then see the services on the computer slow down or they will stop working as you are on them. On the other hand, a DDoS attack will involve a big number of systems that were compromised by a hacker in order to attack one specific target.

While neither of these attacks are used to destroy a security system or to take data, it is often used to generate loss of profit or to make the computer system worthless during use. There may be a loss in connectivity throughout the network and none of the services will work. Depending on the overall goal of the hacker, these attacks can destroy files as programs on the computer.

When one of these attacks is going on, it is similar to noticing that your internet connection is slow. You may feel that the performance of the network is really slow and you are not able to access any of the websites that you want. Luckily, there are a few ways you can see if you are a good target for one of these attacks. If you are getting a lot of spam or a lot of traffic that seems a bit unusual, it may be time to check out some signs of being hacked.

Chapter 4:

Mapping Out Your Hacks

When you start with hacking, you should create a plan of attack. Every hacker needs to have a good idea of what they want to do and where they may find vulnerabilities in the system. Before you start learning some of the strategies that can make hacking successful, lets learn a bit more about how to map out your hacks.

When you are looking to find vulnerabilities, you will not need to check all of the security protocols that are on your devices all at one time. This is just going to make things confusing and sometimes it can cause more problems than it is worth because you will have to deal with too much at once. This means that you need to break up all the testing into parts that are more manageable for you.

Chapter 4: Mapping Out Your Hacks

Many times, it is best to just start with one system or application that you would like to check out first and then slowly go through the list, doing it one at a time, until you reach the end. When determining which system you would like to work on first, ask these questions:

- If your system is attacked, which one would cause the most trouble for you, or which one would be the hardest to fix if you lost it?

- If your system is attacked, which one would be the most vulnerable, therefor the easiest, for the hacker to go after.

- Which parts of the system you are working on are the least documented and may hardly even be checked? Are there any that you have never seen before?

This should make it easier for you to pick which systems you want to work on and you can create the right goals for this process. You should consider keeping some notes along the way to make it easier to get this process done right and so that you can document if there are any issues along the way.

Organizing the Project

When you are ready to run your tests, the devices, applications, and systems that you should check include:

1. Switches and routers

2. Workstations, laptops, and tablets connected to the system

3. Client and server operating systems

4. Database, application, and web servers.

5. Firewalls

6. File, print, and email servers

You may have to run a variety of tests in order to get it all taken care of and how many tests that you run will really depend on the amount of systems and devices that you need to take care of. For example, on a small network, it is easier to test everything without wasting a lot of time in the process. Luckily, when you go through this process, there is some flexibility so you should just choose to spend your time on what seems to make the most sense.

When Should I Hack?

The next question that a lot of people have is when should they start hacking. When you are making your goals, make sure that you plan these tests during times that will cause the smallest amount of disruption for the other users. For example, you should not do testing on the system during the early morning hours if this is the busiest time of day for the business. This not only will slow down the work that other employees will be able to do, but if you run into issues, you may find that you can slow things down even more while figuring it out.

So, make sure to find a time that will not cause too much disruption. Many time doing the tests after hours is best so that you aren't bothering anyone and you have plenty of time to fix mistakes if they happen to come up. Also, before getting started on any of the tests, make sure that everyone else on the system knows about the tests and has information about when you will perform them, how long they will take, and other pertinent information.

What will others see?

To find where the vulnerabilities are in the system, you need look at it from the point of view of a criminal hacker. You are too close to the system and looking at it with fresh eyes can make a difference. You may be used to the system and know how it works inside and out, but the criminal hacker is going to be without some of this knowledge but still with the ability to look at it from a new angle. To figure out what the hacker is seeing, which may be different than what you are seeing, you need to figure out which trails the system is using when someone is on the network.

As a hacker, you have a few options when trying to gather these trails and a good option is to do an online search. For this you need to search about the organization that you are working for. If you want to do tests for your own personal system, just do a search that is related to you. You can then perform a probe and find out what others are able to see about your system. You can use a local port scanner, tools to see what is being shared, and more to catch these issues.

Once you are done with this, there are other searches that you can do online. Take the time to search for:

- Contact details that will point right towards people who are connected with your business. You can do some background checks through ZabaSearch, ChoicePoint, and USSeach.

- Recent press releases about changes in the organization.

- Previous mergers and acquisitions of the company

- SEC documents

- Any trademarks or patents associated with the company.

- Incorporation filings. These are often found through the SEC.

This may take some time, but it gives a good idea of what others are able to see and find out about your company. At times, a simple keyword search is not going to be enough to bring out all the information, so make sure that you do a more advanced search to catch everything. Now that you have an idea of what searchers are able to easily find about the company online, it is time to do a map of the network and look where the vulnerabilities may be.

Mapping out the network

Now you can make your plan on you would like to do the ethical hacking. First, you must have a good idea of what others already know about the system. If it is your personal computer, you should be the only one who knows anything but if you are doing this through work, the network will be much larger as others will get on as well. While most people feel like they have anonymity while online, every time you do a search on your computer, you are leaving little footprints behind that could allow someone in.

A good place to look to see who has access to your network is to look on Whois. This is a tool that is often used to see whether a domain name is available or not, but you can also use it to look at the registration of a particular domain. If your domain is on there, it increases the chance that your contact information and email addresses are already being broadcasted online.

Whois can provide information about DNS servers that are on your domain as well as some details about the tech support of your service provider. Make sure to look at the DNSstuf which will be able to provide information like:

- The information on which host will handle the email for that domain.

- The location of all hosts

- General information about your registration for the domain

- Information about whether this host has been listed as a span host.

There are other sites that you can get this information from and you may want to check out a few different ones to check that your information isn't popping up in other places on the internet. Whois is a great place to get started, but it should not be your ending point.

Google Groups and Forums

Another place that you need to check to make sure your information is secure is through Google groups and forums. These often have a ton of information about your network, often without you having posted it, and can be dangerous for your security. You can sometimes find full qualified domain names, usernames, and IP addresses on here. Doing a simple search through these posts will bring up private information that should never be out there and could expose a lot of your private information.

Luckily, if you find that there is confidential information on one of these sites, it is possible to get it removed. You must have the right credentials to do so, such as working in the IT department of the company whose information is out there. You will then need to go to the support personnel for that Google group or the forum and file a report to get it removed.

Privacy Policies

Your website probably has a privacy policy that will let anyone who gets onto it know the information that you may collect and how it will be protected when they come to the site. While this is good information for the client to know and understand before giving away any personal information, your policy should not go to the extreme of divulging other information that could help out a hacker who is trying to get into the system.

For those who are starting out their website for the first time or who wants to have someone write the privacy policy for them, you should be careful about not broadcasting any personal information about the company and how it works to anyone else. If you put information about your security protocols, for example, or about the firewall in place, you are giving criminal hackers some clues on how to get around it. Even if the privacy policy has been in place for some time, you will still need to go through it and make some changes if it is giving out personal information.

Starting on the system scan

While you are looking for traces of your network online, you are gaining an idea of where hackers will be able to launch their own attacks. You should be looking for any and all places where a hacker could get in by exploiting your vulnerabilities including:

1. Take a look at the information that came up on the Whois search and see how the IP addresses and hostnames can all be laid out. With this site, it is easy to verify all the information and see where a hacker may try to attack your system.

2. Take a bit to scan the internal hosts and see what a possible user may be able to access. Don't forget the possibility that an attacker could come from within the

organization so it is sometimes hard to point out when something is going wrong in house.

3. Check out the system's ping utility. You may need to use a separate third party utility that is able to ping several addresses at the same time. NewScan Tools or SuperScan are great options. If you are unsure about what the gateway IP address is, you can search for it through www.whatismyip.com.

4. You now should do an outside scan of the system by going through all of the open ports. Open up Nmap or SuperScan and check out what others are able to see on the network with a tool like OMnipeek or Wireshark.

These scans are a great way to have an idea of what others are able to see if they are scanning your IP addresses. Without the proper security in place, a hacker can do the same process that you just did and find out about the services that you are running, such as email and web servers, learn the authentication requirements for sharing on the network, and even get on through remote access. You will have to figure out how to block these, but at least you have an idea of what they are able to see at this point.

Find the Vulnerabilities

Once you can see how a hacker will be able to get into the security system, it is easier to figure out how the hacker will want to target the computer. You should consider using some different tools to manage these vulnerabilities. You should always be on the lookout for future vulnerabilities as well; just because they weren't present when you first got started on this process doesn't mean they won't cause issues. Being alert to the system can help you keep your personal, or the company's personal information, safe.

Chapter 5:

Basic Spoofing and Man in the Middle Attack Techniques

Whether you are an ethical hacker or a criminal hacker, there are many different things that you can do to get onto a system. They need to be good at researching and have the patience to wait until a vulnerability shows up in a system or network so that they can make their move. But with some time and work, they will be able to get into the network through a variety of means and make the network collect the information that they want. There are a variety of masquerading and spoofing techniques that will make this a bit easier.

Spoofing

Spoofing is one of the first and best techniques
that a hacker will be able to use. Spoofing is a
technique where a hacker is able to pretend to be
another website, software, organization, or
person. The idea is that the hacker will pretend
to be someone allowed access to the network in
order to get through the security protocols and to
get access to private information that could be
useful to the hacker. The system will believe that
the hacker should be there and the hacker can
just walk through and get whatever they want.
There are several different techniques of
spoofing that a hacker would love to use
including.

IP Spoofing

With this technique, the hacker will be able to
mask their IP address or change it so that the
network is fooled to think that the hacker is a
legitimate user. The hacker could be in another
part of the world and will convince the targeted
network that it is one that can use the system.
The hacker can do this by imitating another IP
address that has met the criteria set up the
network administrator. Once they are on, the
hacker has the ability to take over the network,

44

change files, and so much more without being detected.

This spoof technique is going to work because it is able to find a trusted IP address. Once the trusted IP address is found, the hacker will be able change their headers to fool the network even more so that it feels that the hacker is allowed to be there and they will gain full access. The hacker can look at personal information, change files, and even sent harmful packets to the network without any trace back to the original hacker.

DNS Spoofing

Another spoofing technique is known as DNS spoofing. This method is going to trick a user who is trying to get onto a legitimate site. The hacker will take the IP address and then when a user clicks on it, they will be sent to a malicious website where the hacker has complete control. Sometimes the hacker will take over a legitimate website and turn it to their use, but often they will change around a letter or two to trick people. Users who aren't paying attention or who type in the address wrong will be sent to a bad website and the hacker can take credentials and private information from the user.

Often the user will not realize that they are being tricked. They will get onto the website and figure that it is just where they want to be. They can put in private information, send payment, and more while the hacker is collecting it all privately.

For the hacker to get this to work, they need to have the same LAN as their target. This requires the hacker to search for a weak password on one of the machines that is on the network, something that is possibly even from a different location. Once the hacker accomplishes this, they will be able to redirect all users to their website and easily monitor the activities that are done there.

Email Spoofing

Email spoofing can be useful when a hacker is looking to bypass security of the email. For the most part, email servers are pretty good at recognizing when something is legitimate and when something is spam. Anything that looks like spam or which can be unsafe for your computer will be kept out of the inbox and most people will never see it. But with email spoofing, the hacker is able to bypass the email security and will send you emails that have malicious attachments with them.

Phone Number Spoofing

With phone number spoofing, the hacker will use false phone numbers or area codes in order to mask the identity and location of the hacker. This is really a way for the hacker to get into your voicemail messages or to send out text messages using this spoofed number, or even mislead the target about where the call is located. For example, if the hacker is able to have a number similar to a government office, the target may be willing to hand over personal information.

The biggest issue with these attacks is that most network administrators are not able to easily spot the attacks and the hacker will get to stay on the network and cause a lot of damage in the process. The hacker is able to go through the network easily because of the security protocols and the possibility that the hacker can interact with all the users on the network. The hacker is then able to conduct more man in the middle attacks as well.

Man in the Middle Attacks

The next kind of attack that a lot of hackers will use, and a good follow up after a spoofing attack, is man in the middle attacks. Some hackers will stick with a passive attack and will just be able to view the data and go no further, some will want to do an active attack and cause some more issues.

A man in the middle attack is going to be done when the hacker does an ARP (Address Resolution Protocol), spoofing. With this the hacker is going to send false ARP messages over the network that they took over. When it is pulled off, the fake messages are going to allow the hackers to link in to the IP address of another user, one who is allowed to be on the server. Once the hacker has done this, they will be able to receive all the data that the users are sending over to the IP address the hacker is using.

So basically with this, the hacker is taking over an IP address and making it their own. They will receive all files, communication, and other information that is meant to go to the original user and they can use it however they would like. The hacker has the ability to get onto the network while receiving all traffic that goes on the network as well.

1. Session hijacking—this is when the hacker will use their false ARP to still the user's ID for the session. The hacker will be able to hold on to the information about the

traffic and use it at a later date to get access to the account.

2. Denial of service attack—this is an attack done when the ARP spoof links several IP addresses to the target. During this attack, the data that should be sent to the other IP addresses are sent to one device. This is going to result in an overload of data.

3. Man in the middle attack—with this attack, the hacker is going to pretend that they are non-existent inside the network. Since they are hidden, they are able to modify and intercept messages that are sent between two or more users on the network. The one network may send a legitimate email, but the hacker will take it and change the information to be more malicious before sending it on. The second user will open the malicious information, believing it to be safe.

So how does a hacker go about doing a man in the middle attack or ARP spoofing? Here we will look at one of the ways that a hacker can do this using a tool known as Backtrack, which is really similar to Kali Linux:

Step 1: Do some research

The first thing that the hacker will need to do is find out the data that they need to get started. Using a toll such as Wireshark can help with this. Firing these tools up will allow the hacker to see the traffic that they can connect with through wired or wireless networks and can give them a good starting point.

Step 2: Use a wireless adapter and then place into monitor mode

To get started, take out the wireless adapter and make sure it is on monitor mode. This allows you to see what traffic is going into the connection, even if the traffic shouldn't be there. This method works the best for hubbed networks because there isn't as much security as switched networks.

If you know the types of information that is being sent to the other users on a switch, or you want to bypass it completely, you can attempt to make changes to the entries on the CAM table that will map out the MAC and IP addresses that are sending information to each other. When you change these entries, you can get ahold of the traffic that is meant to go to someone else. For this to work, you will need to do an ARP spoofing attack.

Step 3: Fire up the Backtrack

This is the point where you will bring out the Backtrack software. You will need to pull up the Backtrack and then pull up all three terminals. Next, you will replace the MAC address from the target client with your personal MAC address. The code for doing this is: arpspoof [client IP] [server IP].

Once you do that, you will need to reverse the order of the IP addresses in the string that you just used. This is going to tell the server that your computer is the authorized one so that you are allowed to get onto the system and perform other tasks. You are basically going to become the server and the client so you can receive packets of information and change them how you wish. It also goes the other way around.

For those who are using Linux, you can use the built in feature known as ip_forward, which will make it easier to forward the packets you are receiving. Once you turn this feature on, you will be able to go back into Backtrack and forward these packets with the commandecho 1 >/proc/sys/net/ipv4/ip_forward.

This command is going to make it easier to be right between the client and the server. You will get all the information that goes between these two and as the hacker, you can use the information as you wish. You could look at the system, take personal information, or change anything you want about information that is shared.

Step 4: Check the traffic with Dsniff

Now you will have front row access to all the information being sent on the network. You should use the BackTrack tool to sniff out the traffic and give you a clearer picture. You will need to activate the feature to get it to work.

Step 5: Grab the data and credentials

At this point, you just need to wait to see the client log on to the right server. Once you do this, you are going to be able to see the username and password right in front of you. Since the administrators and the users will use these credentials on all of the computer systems and services, you will be able to use the credentials as well. This will make it simple to get onto the system and see whatever you would like. You are right in the middle of the information, have the credentials to get onto the system, and are pretty much invisible so you as the hacker will have full range mess around with the system and make changes at that time.

Chapter 6:

Hacking Passwords

T he biggest target of hackers is to get passwords, mainly because they are really easy to get. Most people think that they just need to come up with a longer password in order to protect themselves, but there is more to it than that. If the hacker is able to use some of the tricks we stated earlier in this chapter, it does not matter how long your username and password is, they will still have it sent directly to them.

Confidential log in information, including passwords, are considered the weakest links in security because the only thing it relies on is secrecy. Once the secret is out, the security is pretty much gone. This is why it is such a big deal when a big company is hacked and all the username and passwords are leaked. The hacker is now able to get onto the system and use your information however they wish. Sometimes, the user themselves will inadvertently give out their own password for hackers to use.

So how do you hack a password? There are several ways that the hacker can do this including a physical attack, social engineering, and inference. There are also a few different tools that are used to crack passwords including:

1. Cain and Abel—this one is good to help with Windows RDP passwords, Cisco IOS hashes and more.

2. Elmcomsoft Distributed Password Recovery—this one is able to get PGP and Microsoft Office passwords and has been used in order to crack distributed passwords as well as recover up to 10,000 networked computers.

3. Elmcomsoft System Recovery—this has the ability to set administrative credentials, rest expirations on passwords, and reset passwords on Windows computers.

4. Ophcrack—this will use rainbow tables to crack passwords for Windows.

5. Pandora—this can be a good one to use to crack Novell Netware accounts either online or offline.

Some of these tools do have a shortfall because they will require the hacker to have physical access to the system they are hacking. But once the hacker has access to the system that you are protecting, they will be able to dig into all of your encrypted and password protected files with just a few tools.

Often, the hacker is not going to have access to your computer to do a password hack and they will rely on some other tools. Some examples of other methods used to hack a password include:

1. Dictionary attacks—these are attacks that will make use of dictionary words against the password database. This makes it easier to figure out if there is a weak password in the system.

2. Brute force attacks—these are capable of cracking all types of passwords because they are going to use all combinations of numbers, special characters, and letters until the device is cracked. The biggest flaw with this technique is that it can take a ton of time to uncover the password.

3. Rainbow attacks—these are good for cracking any hashed passwords. The tool is really fast compared to others, but it is not able to uncover passwords that are more than 14 characters.

4. Keystroke logging—this is one of the best techniques for cracking a password because it is asking the targeted computer to basically send over the information. The hacker is able to place a recording device on the targeted system to take in all the keystrokes done on the computer. The information is then sent over using programs such as KeyGhost.

5. Searching for weak storages—there are a lot of applications in computers that will store the passwords locally, making them vulnerable to a hacker. When you have physical access to the computer, it is easy to find the passwords through text searches and sometimes they are even stored on the application.

6. Grab the passwords remotely—often it is not possible to physically access a system, it is still possible to get the passwords from a remote location. You will need to

do a spoofing attack first, exploit the SAM file and have the information sent to you.

Once the hacker has access to these passwords, it is easier for them to get the information that they want. They can use the passwords to get onto the network, to get to emails, find out financial accounts, and so much more. You must remember that passwords are a huge vulnerability in your system and to figure out more secure ways to protect your system.

Chapter 7:

Hacking a Network Connection

Another exploit that you can try to take on is hacking a network connection. By doing this, the hacker is able to conceal their identity, enjoy bandwidth for bigger downloads, and have an easy way in to conduct illegal activities. Once the hacker is inside, it is really easy for them to decrypt the traffic for the user and capture them. Just imagine all the different things a hacker is able to do or get ahold of when they are on a Wi-Fi connection and all the trouble the target may have to sort out later.

Before doing a test hack over an internet connection, you must first understand that there are different levels and types of security that are around when protecting the wireless connection. This is going to make a difference on the level and type of attack that could be performed on the network. For example, if you have very little security over the wireless connection, it is not going to take that much work for the hacker to get on the system and do what they want. But for those with more encryption and security, the hacker will have to be a bit craftier before taking over. Some of the basic wireless protocols you may run into:

1. WEP—this stands for wired equivalent privacy and it is designed to provide privacy for those who are on a wired connection. This one is pretty easy to crack because the hacker is easily able to capture the initialized vector. The use of this encryption style is often found on older devise and wireless connections that have not been updated, leaving them more vulnerable to an attack.

2. WPA or WPA1—this protocol was created as one of the ways to address some of the weaknesses present with WEP encryption. It uses the Temporal Key Integrity Protocol to make these improvements without having the user install new hardware on their computers. Pretty much it will use the same security as that found on a WEP connection, but it has

some added bonuses that make it harder to attack.

3. WPA2-PSK—this is used a lot by small businesses and will allow the user to have a pre-shared key, also known as a PSK. This one is a bit more secure than the other two options since there is this added protection, but there are some vulnerabilities.

4. WPA2-AES—this protocol is going to use the Advanced Encryption Standard in order to encrypt data. Most systems that use this will also have a RADIUS service to make it harder to get in. This one is still possible to hack, it just takes a bit longer than the other ones.

Hacking through a WEP Connection

WEP connection is one of the easiest connections to hack through and if you have this kind of connection, you should really run some tests to figure out if you are being hacked or what changes you can make. To do this, the hacker will need a few tools including BackTrack, aircrack-ng, and a wireless adapter. Then to get started:

1. Load up the aircrack-ng inside of BackTrack. You will be able to fire up the BackTrack and then plug in the wireless adapter to find out if it is running. To do this, enter Iwconfi. The program should tell you which adapters it is able to recognize and hopefully yours is on there. You may see other ones, such as wland1 and wlano as well.

2. Take the wireless adapter and put it into promiscuous mode. Now you will be able to see which connections are available. To do this, enter "airmon-ng start wlano". The airmon-ng will then change the name of your interface so it reads momo. You will then have the wireless adapter into monitor mode and simply by entering "airodump-ng mono" you will be able to see all of the access points as well as who is attached to these access points within the range of your adapter.

3. Start capturing your access point. You will need to pick which connection you want to get on and then capture it. You can do this by using the command

a. Airodump-ng –bssid [BSSID of target] -c [channel number] -w WEPcrack momo.

b. Once you enter this command, the BackTrack is going to start capturing packets fro the access point on the right channel. This will send the hacker all the packets that it needs in order to decode any passkeys that are present so they can get onto the wireless. However, it is important to realize that getting these packets will often take some time. If you need to get the packets quickly, it may be time to add in an ARP traffic.

4. Inject the ARP traffic—for anyone who doesn't want to wait around for the packets from WEPkey capture, doing an ARP packet and having it replay can help you get the packets that you need to crack the WEPkey. Since you already have the MAC and BSSID address from the target thanks to doing step 3, you will be able to use them to enter the following command:

a. Aireplay-ng -3 -b [BSSID] – [MAC address] mono

  b. This will allow you to capture the ARPs through the access point of the target. You must keep going in order to capture the IVs that will come in as well.

5. Crack the WEPkey. Once you have the necessary amount of IVs in your WEPcrack file, it is time to run your aircrack-ng. Put in the command:

  a. Aircrack-ng [name of file]

  b. The aircrack-ng will enter the passkey in a hexadecimal format. You will just need to apply this key into your remote access point and then you are on the program. You can use it for free internet, to take over a computer on the system, and much more.

The Evil Twin Hack

The steps above are going to get you onto a wireless network that you are perhaps not allowed to be on. Some hackers may be fine with this because it allows them to get on for free bandwidth that they won't have to pay for. But, there are also other network connection hacks that the hacker ca attempt that will be more powerful while also providing better access to the network rather than just using a free internet connection. One of these powerful hacks is known as the evil twin access point hack.

The evil twin hack is an access point that will act like the access point that a user connects to, but it is manipulative. The target will just see their regular access point and think it is safe to get on, but this manipulative access point is used by a hacker to send the target to the hackers' premade access point, where the hacker can then start a dangerous man in the middle attack.

As a beginner hacker, you may need some practice doing the evil twin attack. Some basic steps to try out include:

1. Turn on BackTrack and start the program airmon-ng. Check to see if your wireless card is running properly by entering bt>iwconfig.

2. Once you have the wireless card, it is time to put it into monitor mode. You will be able to od this by entering the command bt >airmon-ng start wlan0.

3. Now you need to fire up the airdump-ng. you will start capturing the wireless traffic that your wireless card is able to detect.

To do this, enter the command bt >airodump-ng mono. After this step, you will have the ability to see all access points that are in range and can pick out the one that belongs to your target.

4. You will need to wait for when the target connects. Once the target gets onto the access point, you can copy the BSSID and the MAC address that you want to hack into.

5. Now the hacker will need to create an access point that has the same credentials.

   a. First, pull up a new terminal and type in bt > airbase-ng -a [BSSID] —essid ["SSID of target] -c [channel number] mono

   b. This is going to create the access point that you want. It will look the same as the original access point so the target will click on it, but it puts the hacker right in the middle as the one in control.

6. De-authenticate the target—for the target to get onto your new access point, you will need to get them off the one they are connected to. Since many wireless

connections will go with 802.11, everyone who is connected to the access point will be de-authenticated when you do this. When the target tries to get back on to the internet, they will connect automatically to the one with the strongest signal, which in this case will be your manipulated access point.

    a. To get the target off their access point, make sure to do the following command: bt > aireplay-ng –deauth 0 -a [BSSID of target]

7. Turn the signal of the evil twin up. The trick on this one is to get the fake access point to have a strong signal. It needs to be at least as strong, but preferably stronger, than the original point of access. This can be tricky because you are likely further away than the original access point.

    a. Iwconfig wlan0 txpower 27 will help you to turn up the signal on your access point.

    b. This can add 500 milliwatts to your power. If you are too far away though, this may not be enough. You either need to be closer to the target or consider a newer wireless card that is able to go up to 2000 milliwatts.

8. Put the evil twin to good use—once you have established the evil twin and you know that the target and the network are all connected to it, it is time to take the steps needed in order to detect all the activities going on in the system. It often depends on what you want to do with the system for where you will go from here.

   a. There are a lot of options of what to do at this point. Hackers who have gone and created an evil twin are interested in more than just free wireless so they will often do man in the middle attacks, intercept traffic, add in new traffic, or steal information from the system, often without the target realizing.

Hacking through a network connection can give a hacker a lot of possibilities. Some choose to just do this for the free bandwidth when they want to download a lot of information and they either don't have internet or don't have enough to do the work. But there are many hackers who will get on these internet connections in the hopes of causing some mischief and damage. Either way, it is important to learn how to protect your internet connection to keep your personal information safe from any hackers.

Chapter 8:

Popular Tools for Hacking

Whether you are a criminal or ethical hacker, there are many great tools that you can use to help protect your personal system, help protect a larger system, or attack a system. These tools are going to help to make things easier and can help you to find the vulnerabilities in the system. Many of them are crowd-sourced through the internet and you can look through forums and other hubs online that are devoted to hackers.

As an ethical hacker, you should use some of the common tools to detect these vulnerabilities, administer hacks, and even conduct tests. Some of the most popular hacking tools you can use either as a criminal or ethical hacker include:

Ipscan or Angry IP Scanner

The IP scanner is used to figure out what the IP address for a target computer is so that the hacker can track them It can snoop through the network ports to check for any gateways that make it easier to get into the targeted system. It is not just used by criminal hackers since system administrators and engineers will be able to check for any vulnerabilities in their personal systems.

An ipscan can be used across various platforms because it is open source and it is praised for being a really effective hacking tool. Most beginner hackers will start out with this tool because it is easy to use and really efficient.

Kali Linux

This application is relatively new, coming out during 2015, and is a favorite with hackers because of all the great features that come with it. This is a toolkit that is centered around security and you will be able to run it through the USB or a CD without having to install it on the computer. The toolkit will be able to work on most of the interfaces that you will need for hacking including cracking Wi-Fi passwords and creating spoof messages and fake networks.

Cain and Abel

As one of the biggest manufacturers of computers and software system, the Microsoft brand is trusted by millions of users. Cain and Abel is a hacking toolkit that will work against Microsoft operating systems and can be used by criminal hackers to get through the system or by ethical hackers in order to protect systems that are using these operating systems.

There is a lot that you can do with this tool. You can recover passwords for your wireless network, user account passwords and it is possible to use some forcing methods in order to crack the passwords. Some will use the Cain and Abel program in order to record their VoIP conversation sessions.

Burp Suite

For those who are looking to find vulnerabilities in their websites or networks, Burp Suite can make it easier. This tool will look at each cookie that is present on a website and can allow the hacker to start connections inside the website applications.

There are a several methods to try to accomplish this. For criminal hackers, they will use a Burp Suite to examine the cookies on the website in order to figure out where the holes in security are so you are able to take advantage. Criminal hackers will be able to start their own connections on the website to make it collect information or run applications that they want to be in control. On the other hand, ethical hackers can look at how the website works and find vulnerabilities that are there to keep it safe.

Ettercap

Another tool that is really efficient is Ettercap. This one is used by hackers who would like to launch man in the middle attacks. The whole idea is to is to convince two systems that they are talking to each other, but the hacker is in the middle as a relay person. One system may send a message, but the hacker will take over the message and relay something different. This is a great tool that helps to steal or manipulate transactions so that the data is transferred differently between the systems. It is also a great way to eavesdrop on conversations between the networks.

John the Ripper

When it comes to using brute force to crack passwords and get into a system, the John the Ripper tool is one of the best. Many hackers don't like using brute force because these tactics can sometimes take too much time, but Jack the Ripper is one of the most efficient if you are trying to recover passwords that have been encrypted. It is a good way for new hackers to start with finding passwords and getting onto a new network or can be added to your other choices to get into the network.

Metasploit

This tool is widely celebrated among hackers because it is really efficient at helping an ethical hacker. Metasploit will be a good way to help identify security issues that may be present in the network. Beginner hackers can use this as a network planning tool to check if someone is on their network, if they are authorized, and where a criminal hacker may try to get on to the network.

Aircraft-ng and Wireshark

These tools are often used together in order to hack into user passwords and IDs and to find the wireless connections through Wi-FI. Wireshark will be the sniffer in the packet in order to find where the wireless connection is and the Aircraft-ng will capture the information so that you can get onto the network. There are a lot of other tools that are available in both suites to allow you to monitor the security of your Wi-Fi connection.

These are just a few of the tools that you can use to help get started with hacking, whether you are working as an ethical hacker or a criminal hacker. It is important to keep up on the industry to find out which new products are coming out. Even as an ethical hacker, you need to look on hacking blogs and forums in order to find out which new tools are coming out. If you aren't looking and keeping up with the new tools, a criminal hacker will use them against you. There are always new tools that are coming up and they can make it easier to find vulnerabilities in your system and to protect yourself and your network.

Chapter 9:

How to Hack a Website

O ne popular place that hackers like to attack is websites. They are able to get onto a website and then when someone else comes to visit what looks like a legitimate site, they will be able to attack the computer. Here we will look at a few of the attacks that are available when trying to take over a website.

Directory traversal attack

The directory is basically the folder that the web designer would have used in order to store the files for the website. This means that a directory traversal attack is when the hacker is able to get into this directory and navigate through all of the files that are inside. There are a few sensitive files for your website that can be located in these directories include the confi, htaccess, and root files.

Now, if you want to be able to get access to a text file, let's say that it is called abcdefg.txt and it is located in the directory file called John, you would need to type the command "....abcdefg" in order to move to the area where it is stored. Notice that there are four dots that are in front of it to ensure that you are able to move up two folders (the two dots is just to move up one folder and then the four dots would be to move up two folders).

A directory traversal attack is going to be an HTTP exploit that is aimed at getting ahold of some files that are restricted or even viewing some random files that are on the webs server, such as the SSL private keys and the password files. Most of the time, hackers are usually going to want to get into the root directory of the server, and with the help of the dot slash technique, they will be able to do this. This is a vulnerability that many web servers need to work on to keep the web servers safe.

A hacker is able to perform searches in order to figure out which types of files are considered publicly accessible inside of the website directory. The hacker may want to use the HTTrack website copier, which is a spider program, that is able to find all of the files that are publicly accessible. This tool is free to use and really easy since you will just need to load it up, give the project a name, and then instruct the software which website it needs to mirror. It may take up to a few hours, but the HTTrack will be able to show you all of the records and files that the website will contain and will make sure that they are all stored inside of your drive C: My Websites.

Many of the sites that you will check out will contain information that is sensitive and shouldn't be viewed publicly, such as the source codes and even the application scripts. You should take some time to watch out for any .rar or lzip files in the websites servers. Even pdf and .html files can contain some of this sensitive information that the hacker would want to get ahold of.

Another way that the hacker is able to search through to find some public files is to go through Google. You will be able to bring out the advanced queries in Google in order to expose some of the sensitive information, as well as webcams, critical server directors, credit card numbers and more. This is because whenever Google goes through and searches a website, it is going to store all of these records in files that are in its cache, making them easy for hackers to find. In fact, these are even easier to use because the hacker doesn't need to mirror a specific website and then manually search through the files to find what they want.

There are a few queries that you are able to use in Google in order to get the information that you want including:

- Site:hostname keywords: when you use this query, Google is going to search for any keyword that you want. You could type in the keyword or the website that you want to get the information that you would like. For example, you could tpe in something like site: www.bigmoneyspeaker.com credit card and see what Google has in store for you.

- Filetype: file-extension site: hostname: when you are using this query, Google is going to look for a type of file on the website that you want to target. You can look for db, rar, pdf, zip, and doc files based on what you would like to find. A good example of how to write this out includes filetype: pdf site: www.madhatter.com.

These are just a few types of operators that you are able to use in order to get the information that you want out of your website. This is why it is so important for you to be careful with the information that you are putting online because if the website is not careful with your information, the hackers will be able to get ahold of it when they want.

Protecting your directory

It is up to the website developer to make sure that they are protecting the website from these types of attacks. There are three countermeasures that are the most successful with these issues including:

- Avoid storage private, confidential, or old records on the service. You want to make sure that only the DocumentROot or the htdocs folder is only containing the files that are needed in order to make the website run properly. You should also make sure that the files never contain any information that is sensitive.

- Prevent Google and some other search engines from going onto the site and storing data that is sensitive into their cache. You are able to do this by configuring your robots.txt file.

- You can also make sure that the web server you use is configured to only allow certain directories to be accessible by the public. You can also set up a minimum privileges to help control how much public access there is and then only allows access to the directories that is needed to help the site run the right way.

Another option that you may want to consider is to use the Google Hack Honeypot. This is a tool that is able to attract malicious hackers while you get a chance to see how they are hacking into your site. You will then be able to make some changes to ensure that they stay away from your website by putting in the right countermeasures.

Hackers are often looking for ways to get onto a website and get personal information from the clients that are on that website or to use it as a way to attack others who come through and use the website. Learning how the hacker is able to make the attack and then using the right countermeasures will ensure that your website stays safe and that the hackers never reach any personal information that may be stored on there.

Conclusion

Thank you for purchasing this book!

I hope this book was able to help you to understand more about hacking and how it is not all black and white hat like most people think. There are different worlds when it comes to hacking and while the media may portray it as something bad and sinister, there are many applications where you can use it in your life to do some good, or at least in a way that won't cause mischief.

The next step is to start putting some of the techniques and strategies that you learned to work. These are meant to help you out as a beginner, someone who may have a love of computers but who hasn't had a chance to figure out hacking on their own. They are not the only means of hacking that you can use, but they will give you a practical place to start on your journey.

Additionally, please visit our Amazon Author page for more great info and resources.

Conclusion

You will find all the books you need to learn about:

Python Programming, SQL, JavaScript, and even **TOR** if that's something you fancy!!

Last but not least, if you enjoyed this book and thought it was helpful, we certainly won't say no to a 5-star **review on Amazon**.

Thank You and Best of Luck in Your Hacking Endeavors!!!